THE GUN

THE GUN II: THE DRAMA CONTINUES

THE GUN III: KEEP IT MOVING

THE GUN IV: NOW

THE GUN V: WILL NEVER

THE GUN VI: MORE KNOWLEDGE

THE GUN VII: PARTNERS

THE GUN VIII

THE GUN IX

THE GUN X: THE DRAMA STILL CONTINUES

THE GUN XI: COMMUNITIES AND NEIGHBORHOODS

THE GUN XII: LEGEND

THE GUN XIII: PROTEST AGAINST

THE GUN XIV: STILL HERE

THE GUN XV: THE TIME HAS COME

THE GUN XVI: DISHARMONY

THE GUN XVII: CAUSING

THE GUN XVIII: IN THE 21ST CENTURY

THE GUN IXX: DISHARMONY II

THE GUN XX: RAPID FIRE AKA ASSAULT RIFLE

GUN VIOLENCE AND CRIME

FOREWARD

Young Dave Queeley was a victim of society. He fell into the traps that many of our youth are facing today, and he paid the price. He is the perfect voice for, and to, the kids in our community. He's allowed to talk the talk, because he has walked the walk. If you want to know what can happen when you hook up with thugs, and become one, he can tell you. It's not a pretty story, but it is one that needs to be heard.

As the Director of the St. John Community Foundation, I have had the pleasure of interacting with Dave Queeley in the many roles he plays here in the Virgin Islands. The Dave Queeley I know is no victim. He is a survivor. He believes love will triumph over hate, and if you allow his words to penetrate the fog of denial, you will too.

A 2013 report by the International Centre for Prison Studies, ranked the United States as the country with the highest per capita number of its population in jail, and placed the USVI in the number four spot. Dave Queeley is no stranger to the issues that plague our community. He has opinions, insight and solutions to many of our problems. I join a multitude of people in this community who have heard and been moved by his words.

Mr. Queeley is a prolific writer. He writes, and writes, and then keeps writing. He writes about good things and bad. His writing can make you laugh. It can make you cry. It can make you mad, and it is meant to. Mad enough to take action. He is a protestor speaking against everything from guns and gangs, to cheating and toxic food. He is a community activist, fighting for love, respect, honor and loyalty.

He is a real friend to the community. As a change agent, his essays and oratories speak boldly about what is really going on, whether we choose to see it or not. He is a generous volunteer, from working in the schools to the community garden.

He is a real friend to our youth. Mr. Queeley is a mentor who has proven to be consistent and reliable. He knows how to talk to our youth, and more importantly, he knows how to listen to them. They listen too, as he tells them about self respect, self control, pride and how to become the leaders that we need them to be.

He is a real friend to the authorities. As a volunteer for the Juvenile Wrap Around Program, and in the schools, he motivates and encourages youth not to fall victim to society's dark side. He continues to lay the groundwork for overcoming negativity, violence and injustice. His words shed light on the right path.

He is a real friend to me. I am honored on so many levels to be able to support Mr. Queeley in all his endeavors, because they add value to this community and will leave a legacy of good intentions for future generations to follow. I am glad you have this book in your hands, it will make a difference in your life.

Sincerely, Celia Kalousek
Director St. John Community Foundation

THE GUN

By
Dave R. Queeley

THE GUN has never had a funeral or gotten buried. It's always alive.

THE GUN doesn't go on trial for murder or for robbery. It's always the partner who goes on trial all the time, not the gun.

It's made far away so how did they get here to cause so much mental and spiritual havoc in our communities and neighborhoods?

THE GUN makes some people feel like they are super heroes with special powers
And has taken a whole lot of people's lives.

It has caused a whole lot of people to get a life sentence in the pit of doom and injustice, which is jail or prison.

THE GUN is Satan the Devil's greatest invention of self destruction.

It has never killed anyone alone. It always needs a partner to help pull the trigger.

THE GUN is never a role model of love, justice, and most of all good intentions and it's now
More valuable than life. Life is now worthless.

THE GUN is a partner that has no soul, but it continues to take souls every day.

It's the King of Kings and Lord of Lords of self destruction and death and it's
Only affiliated with hopelessness, disrespect, dishonor and disunity.

THE GUN has no traditional values or moral qualities to it.

THE GUN has no safety net around it, it's just free falling head first, straight into eternal hell fire and it has caused the homicide rate in our communities and neighborhoods to be among the highest in the world.

In the 21st century it is now teaching our children and young people how to live fast and die young.

THE GUN is not used to bring or create life, but it's used as a tool to take a life.

It does not bring mental and spiritual respect, honor or peace; it only brings self destruction and death.

The time has come to put down **THE GUN** because jail or prison is a male room. Only males coming in and going out on a daily basis.

The time has come to put down **THE GUN** and pick up a book.

Read a good book over picking up THE GUN!

THE GUN PART II
THE DRAMA CONTINUES
By
Dave R. Queeley

The only gun young people and children now need in their holster is love, justice and good intentions.

THE GUN has caused fist fights to go out the window of life. Now it's all about the use of automatic weapons to settle any argument or dispute.

THE GUN does not mourn the loss of any lives its partner takes. It is now public enemy number one and it's the new energizer bunny; it keeps on going and going.

It has turned some young people and children into blood thirsty war mongers who do not care about any consequences. It has caused the homicide rate and violent crime rate to explode and that's not positive news.

Some young and old people are mentally and spiritually lost because THE GUN has grown to epic heights with no solution or end in sight.

THE GUN has no inspirational values or vision to it. It makes some boys feel like men and over confident that they can do anything they want, in the 21st century.

They now have no consciousness and this has caused the incarceration rate among colored and Latino males to be off the charts.

THE GUN has no positive signal to it; it only has a negative signal that leads to self destruction and death.

It is now the new Messiah to some young and old people and it now shows the coward in all its partners when they pull the trigger.

THE GUN will always remain the drama queen or king in some people, young and old lives. That's why the drama continues on a daily basis. This is an addiction that some people, young and old can't break free of; going to the rehab would not help.

It has caused the decline in the authority of respect, love, justice, and good intentions and has caused hopelessness, disrespect, dishonor and disunity to enslave some young and old people from the cradle to the grave.

THE GUN will never help people, young and old emancipate their minds from spiritual and mental slavery. It will never promote and support love, respect and good intentions around the world.

THE GUN will never have any universal truth to it. The only universal truth is THE GUN is all about self destruction and death happening in the 21st century.

THE GUN is the only serial killer who has never been convicted.

THE GUN

04-13-2012
Friday the 13th

THE GUN PART III

KEEP IT MOVING

By

Dave R. Queeley

THE GUN is the new Disneyland of self destruction and death. It has never and will never bring anyone back from the grave, even after they have been shot and killed by its partner.

It now has teenagers being charged as adults for murder which is a sad story that continues to occur in the twenty first century. It remains unindicted for being the co-conspirator of all the random, senseless and unnecessary shootings and killings that continue to proliferate on a regular basis.

In our communities and neighborhoods, which we cherish, THE GUN has established itself as a god that has corrupted the minds, bodies and souls of our young people and children, including those irresponsible adults.

It will always bring bad karma all the time, there will never be any good karma coming from THE GUN. It has empowered evil minds to enslave and oppress our young people and children of color to ensure that the inferiority complex syndrome remains as an icon.

THE GUN is systematically slaughtering our future generation with no real end in sight, just because of their motto, "NO SNITCHING". Some people, young and old are on the dead end road of life.

It is the number one idol that is being worshipped by some people, young and old on a regular basis. It is always a symbol of death and self destruction; nothing good happens when you use a gun.

THE GUN will never keep peace, freedom, unity and the truth moving. It continues to have some people, young and old disregard having the authority of respect, love, justice and good intentions as an everyday thing in their lives.

It is now the Book of Life to some people, young and old in the 21st century. It has brain washed some people, young and old into believing the false notion that evil will conquer good intentions.

THE GUN and its' partner have a marriage of convenience; no love or respect for one another. It's now a serious hurdle with a barrier We the People must overcome, if we ever want to see peace, freedom and unity happen in this life.

It has been tormenting the whole world for centuries and has become so widespread that it will be hard to stop it from continuing to destroy the mind, body and soul of young people and children. THE GUN cannot save mankind from self destruction and death, only the Creator's love can do that.

It will never collapse without a true fight from the authority of respect, love, justice and good intentions.

THE GUN invasion is on and it's getting out of control. It's one of the world's most dangerous tools created by mankind and it will never build a future, only destroy it.

THE GUN is always guilty until its proven innocent!

THE GUN

THE GUN PART IV

NOW

By

Dave R. Queeley

THE GUN is now a green eyed evil monster that is slowly destroying our communities and neighborhoods. They now need help from the Avengers and Super Friends to help destroy this green eyed evil monster.

It is now a phenomenon that also afflicts many other parts of society. It's now trying to annihilate an entire generation of young people and children.

In the 21st century it now has its own moral code that does not include having respect, love, justice and good intentions. The only moral code it now has is kill or be killed.

Some people, young and old are jumping out of the frying pan and into the fire. THE GUN now has an unpredictable temper that continues to lead to its partner's unpredictable violent outburst.

It is now the new Renaissance Man to some young people and children in the 21st century.

THE GUN is now a serious plague without any cure insight, so the catastrophe continues to live on. It is now the boss of all bosses when it comes to social disorder. It has now invaded our communities and neighborhoods like a cancerous growth that now needs surgery to be removed.

THE GUN now has some people, young and old brain damaged or dead and starving for the truth. It will never help or let them regain any consciousness about the Creator's original plan which is, "Good will conquer evil and Love will triumph over hate."

In the 21st century it now has caused the decline of the authority of respect, love, justice and good intentions from being young and old people's top and highest priority in life.

THE GUN now has young people, children and some old people being their own worst enemy because of their self destructive behavior and attitudes. It now has young people, children and some old people continuing to struggle in the escape from the evil spirits or demons that makes them trigger happy.

It's now a betrayer of all its partners who pull the trigger. In the 21st century it's now easier to find a gun than a job. It is now the new petri dish for materialism, hopelessness, disrespect, dishonor and disunity continue to grow.

THE GUN now has young people, children and some old people backsliding from the Creator's original plan and not following the Laws of Creation to the fullest.

THE GUN now has all temptations down pack and it continues to play on young people, children and some old people's weakness of the mind, body and soul. It now has some young and old people refusing to abandon their lifestyle of doing what is wrong and negative.

It's now some people, young and old D.O.C., also known as Drug of Choice. It is now a very big thorn in the side and the crown of thorns on the head of our communities and neighborhoods.

It is now a saboteur and mastermind of all the dirty tricks that leads to self destruction and death and it now has a license to slaughter anything living, animals or human beings.

THE GUN is now the world's most notorious trouble maker since it was invented. It continues participating in all the violent crimes that now happens in the twenty first century.

THE GUN is now like a piranha fish very aggressive and deadly.

THE GUN PART V
WILL NEVER
By
Dave R. Queeley

THE GUN will never be obliterated from the world, mankind will always use the excuse, "We need it for protection".

It will never let young people, children and some old people manifest the Creator's Words of Wisdom, original plan and follow the Laws of Life to move forward to the true presentation of Creation. "GOOD OVER EVIL."

In the 21st century THE GUN does not know anything about loyalty and humbleness; it only knows about how to cause misery, injustice and disunity to happen.

THE GUN will never promote more life, more love and more unity; it only promotes more bloodshed, more self destruction and more death.

It will never give its partners a hug much less say "I love you", and will never have unconditional love for its partners. THE GUN love will wear off the moment its partner pulls the trigger.

It will never change its moral code of life which is kill or be killed; and
will never help improve the mental and spiritual tension in our communities and neighborhoods. It only makes things worst.

THE GUN will never be a confidence builder, it's always self centered and selfish, and it will never protect the environment, it only will help to continue to destroy it.

It will never stop causing atrocities around the world. It's a tool of death and oppression.

THE GUN will never have the obligation to prevent violent crimes from ever happening again.

It will never notify any law enforcement officers when a violent crime is going down. THE GUN will never call 911, and will never testify in court, it's always "La Costa Nostras" silence is key.

It will never cease fire or accept any truce. THE GUN will never have a moment of silence for all the victims its partner has killed.

It will never have any self discipline to it and will never fully release its grip on young people, children and some old people's mind, body and soul any time soon.

In the 21st century it will never give up its reputation as a parent's worst nightmare. The death of a child from gun violence is a nightmare.

THE GUN will never accelerate the return to having respect, love, justice and good intentions back into young people and children's lives as a top priority.

It will never give up its duties of carrying out Satan the Devil's genocidal plan of self destruction and death,

And will never lead its partner to the promise land of respect, love, justice and good intentions. The only promise land THE GUN knows is self destruction, misery and death.

It will never stick with its partner through thick and thin, the first sign of trouble they are out of Dodge City.

THE GUN will never get convicted but it comes close when it gets seized by the police.

THE GUN PART VI

MORE KNOWLEDGE

By

Dave R. Queeley

"More knowledge about THE GUN continues to be written."

THE GUN will swallow up its partner as long as they continue to do what's wrong and negative in life.

THE GUN will always be the greatest demonstration of friendly fire in the history of the world. Look how much innocent people have died by the actions of its partner when they pull the trigger. THE GUN is now the apple of young people, children and some old people's eyes. THE GUN will one day exterminate them from the world; as it continues to be the apple of their eyes.

It is now destroying the soul of humanity and is never honorable, cautious and sensitive. It's a big hindrance to the return of the authority of respect, love, justice, and good intentions in our communities and neighborhoods on a daily basis.

In the 21st century it's a deceptive tool that young people, children and some old people cannot seem to get enough of. It's now like candy to them. It will never bless anyone who worships or obeys the Laws of Life. THE GUN only brings sorrow, distress, spiritual and mental calamity.

It will never let young people and children learn the art of prioritizing and will never be merciful or let goodness and truth be present in large numbers. It will always deprive its partner of the chance to be godly.

THE GUN is hard to comprehend because it shows no appreciation for the Creator's original plan and for following the Laws of Creation.

It will never generate the divine power of peace and unity. THE GUN is now the only desirable treasure or jewel young people, children and some old people want in their life 24 hours/7 days of the week.

THE GUN will never let young people and children who own one have a clear perception of the truth, doing what's right and being a positive person. THE GUN is never harmless. But love, justice, and good intentions will help free the mind, body and soul of young people and children from the evil influence or effects of THE GUN.

It is the headmaster and teacher at the evil institution of disrespect, dishonor, and disunity. This institution will never teach its partners about good intentions and self control. THE GUN does not have any heavenly origin about it. The Creator clearly did not bring it into existence. It's the angel named Lucifer also known as Satan the Devil's evil enterprise number one commodity of destruction for sale to the highest bidder.

It will never let young people and children pay attention to the complete picture of life which is "Good will conquer evil and Love will triumph over hate", all the time. THE GUN is now a dignitary or celebrity young people and children will do almost anything to be near, day or night.

It has caused our communities and neighborhoods to lose several degrees of freedom, peace, and unity. It now has them having their priorities of life backwards.

THE GUN will never let young people and children who are obsessed with it, fulfill their true purpose for being on this earth which is to be positive energy and to glorify the Creator that is within them.

It now has some young people and children not able to go a whole day without thinking about it or the selfish ways that leads to anguish and depression after they have pulled the trigger of self-destruction and death, not about the recovery of the authority of respect, love, justice and good intentions in their lives.

This recovery will stop the GUN's power from continuing to rise. Seek more knowledge and PUT DOWN THE GUN.

THE GUN PART VII
PARTNERS
By
Dave R. Queeley

THE GUN and its partners are now true obstacles and barriers to peace, freedom and unity in our communities and neighborhoods. THE GUN and its partners will never be law abiding citizens. THE GUN and its partners have made an already vulnerable population even more desperate to find true solutions to gun violence and crime.

They are now taking human life every other second worldwide and will continue to end up in three places, the hospital, jail or prison and the cemetery if they continue doing what's wrong and negative in life. They will never restore law and order in our communities and neighborhoods.

They are now morally, spiritually, and mentally BANKRUPT in the twenty first century and continue swinging from the chandelier of hopelessness, disrespect, dishonor, and disunity on a daily basis.

THE GUN and its partners do not always kill their victims they sometimes paralyze them for life.

They now lack the proper understanding and discipline about consequences of their actions when they pull the trigger and will continue setting and breaking records for murder so the incarceration rate will continue to be off the charts. If anyone needs proof all they have to do is buy and read a news paper or turn on the T.V. or radio and you will see or hear the proof.

THE GUN and its partners don't give a damn about any consequences. They are now neck deep in the waters of disrespect, dishonor, and disunity which are the offspring of injustice, misery, and planned doom.

They are never weary of the daily deterioration of life, they continue to cause on a regular basis and will never understand the powers of love, justice and good intentions.

THE GUN and its partner will never have words of encouragement to tell young people and children to stay away from the pit of doom and injustice which is jail or prison and it has no good stories to tell about life, it's always something about destruction and death.

They will continue to always unanimously reject any motion to cease fire. Cease fire will be challenging their power of authority and will never cooperate with the police unless they have proof that a crime has been committed.

THE GUN and its partner now have a shoot first mentality, and asking a question comes later. In the 21st century they never take a look in the mirror of life and stop pretending they live in the world all alone.

They will never help bring back happiness, respect and unity to our communities and neighborhoods. They have forgotten that love, justice and good intentions have the power to heal the world from evil spirits.

THE GUN and its partners will not take advantage of the opportunities that life has to offer them to do what's right and positive. They are now too busy worshipping idols and will never have any confidence, hope and aspirations to seeing peace, freedom and unity happen in our communities and neighborhoods.

THE GUN and its partner will never know anything about the infinity of love, respect and good intentions.

THE GUN and its partner must never forget the time has come to live consciously.

THE GUN

THE GUN VIII

By

Dave R. Queeley

These words of THE GUN will become iconic.

THE GUN will never let young people, children and some old people interact respectfully with one another. It's now the new religion of some people, young and old.

It is now the only church some people, young and old will attend where Satan the Devil also known as the angel Lucifer is the messiah of kill or be killed.

And it will never prevent violent crimes from happening in the future. THE GUN now has an out of control ego that now demands special treatment from its partners. NO QUESTIONS ASKED.

THE GUN's ancestry is always self destruction, misery and death and will always partake and promote any promiscuous ways that leads to self destruction and death. It's never cordial and respectful to anyone.

It will always be its partner's friend as long as they are doing what is wrong and negative, the moment they pull the trigger. It becomes their enemy, because it's the father of all weapons of mass destruction, disrespect, dishonor and disunity.

THE GUN is not something you want to have a relationship with. It is the new gold-digger of young people and children's mind, body and most of all soul. For some of them this is the best thing that ever happened in their entire life, which they have not yet lived.

In the 21st century it's now depriving our communities and neighborhoods of the respect, love, justice and good intentions they deserve. THE GUN now has hope; doing what's right and being positive is fading away fast from our communities and neighborhoods vocabulary. It now has so many enemies all around the world who would like to see it destroyed.

THE GUN and its partner have a roller coaster marriage that always ends up suffering from a violent and sometimes fatal blow to the head.

It now has all kinds of evil skeletons in its closet. THE GUN's closet is called a graveyard.

It now has so many victims who was killed by its partner that it will take decades to tell all of them R.I.P.

It has caused so much hatred and confusion among young people and children. This hatred and confusion has caused them to start fighting and slaughtering one another with no true end in sight and is now the new axis of evil that has invaded our communities and neighborhoods, that will devour them in the future if they continue to hang around on a regular basis.

THE GUN is never shy and ashamed about helping its partner attack and kill anyone in its path that wants to stop them from being negative and doing what's wrong in life.

They will never surrender to love, justice and good intentions. THE GUN will never let its partner begin to cultivate a positive lifestyle. It will always discourage that from happening.

It has never made mankind happy. There is nothing about THE GUN's ancestry that will produce happiness and unity.

It is never a blessing, it's always a mental and spiritual curse to the young people and children who are mentally and spiritually dead, who do not care about Creations wrath.

THE GUN is now the chief in the new city of Sodom and Gomorrah where sin and iniquity rules with an iron fist.

THE GUN

THE GUN IX

By

Dave R. Queeley

Today the spotlight shines more brightly on THE GUN so here is the 411.

THE GUN will never let young people and children balance their inner connection to the universe and the authority of respect, love, justice and good intentions. It will always have young people and children's personalities clashing all the time.

It's a villain that has put fear, disrespect, hopelessness and disunity in the hearts and minds of young people and children and will never divorce its partners as long as they keep doing what's wrong and negative in life.

THE GUN will always have its partner's life in mental and spiritual shambles. It will always seem like it is competing for the love, honor and respect of its partners.

In the 21st century it now has its partners forgetting that LIFE IS TOO SHORT TO BE NEGATIVE. THE GUN is not something you can put your trust in. It's never a crisis fixer. It's now the new Dr. Jekyll and Mr. Hyde in our communities and neighborhoods.

THE GUN will never motivate its partner to seek to know the truth about the Creator's original plan, which is GOOD WILL CONQUER EVIL AND LOVE WILL TRIUMPH OVER HATE.

It's getting a lot more exposure than it could ever imagine with all those random, senseless and unnecessary killings and shootings now happening in the twenty first century.

It's the new culture war that is now going on in our communities and neighborhoods. It will never reimburse anyone whose life its partner has taken in the battle of good intentions over evil.

THE GUN now has young people and children mentally and spiritually imprisoned in their own minds, because it has no guidelines for the use of love, justice and good intentions. It only has evil guidelines that lead to self destruction, misery and death. THE GUN continues to telepathically speak to its potential partners or aggressors that, evil will conquer good and hate will triumph over love. Sometimes they believe it and pull the trigger of self destruction and death.

It has cemented itself and taken the position as the true destroyer of peace, freedom and unity in young people and children's lives on a regular basis. It is certainly not flawless and it lacks any natural or godly connection to love, respect and good intentions.

THE GUN has an unprecedented momentum that continues to lead young people and children to self destruction, misery and death. It is the number one promoter of mass murder, disrespect, dishonor and disunity.

It's the gas that has fueled the mental and spiritual genocide that is now taking place in our communities and neighborhoods on a daily basis.

THE GUN now has the cemetery full of young people and children who have lost their lives carelessly. It will never let young people and children rely on each other for the mental and spiritual support and growth they need to be a positive person in life.

THE GUN and its partner will never be a part of the generosity and spirit of love, respect and good intentions.

It's now a true success story of self destruction, mental, spiritual and physical death of young people and children. In the twenty first century it is used and endorsed by the evil members of organized injustice and planned doom.

THE GUN is now like aggressive sand fleas or mosquitoes that would not go away.

It now has our communities and neighborhoods on the brink of mental and spiritual extinction on a daily basis.

**Today the spotlight shines brightly on THE GUN.
The time has come to PUT IT DOWN and stop leaving love, respect and good intentions at home.**

THE GUN

THE GUN X
THE DRAMA STILL CONTINUES
By
Dave R. Queeley

THE GUN will always remain the messiah in some people, young and old lives. That's why the drama still continues to happen on a daily basis.

THE GUN is costing our communities and neighborhoods their sanity and soul. It's now the new megatron to young people and children who are hopeless and will never help with the re-establishment of the authority of respect, love, justice and good intentions in our communities and neighborhoods.

It's now causing murder season to now be every day with no end in sight. THE GUN is now a public relations nightmare for any society that wants to see the Creator's original plan fulfilled and the Laws of Creation followed on a daily basis.

THE GUN is a shining object that glitters all the time and it has distracted the masses from having respect, love, justice and good intentions in their lives.

It's like an S.T.D. that We the People need a cure for badly. THE GUN is the number one fraudster of all its partners and it's the real Occupy Movement because it's now everywhere, even in church.

It is now the number one import in our communities and neighborhoods, and is now a real leach on our communities and neighborhoods and its sucking the blood and life out of them.

THE GUN is always disobedient and undisciplined and will never let love, justice and good intentions be possible in our communities and neighborhoods, with all those random, senseless and unnecessary killings and shootings continuing to happen.

It's time to put THE GUN on the front of the dollar bill because that's all some people now put their trust in and not in the Creator. The stress and anxiety it has caused in our communities and neighborhoods is like acid being poured all over the body.

THE GUN is Satan's number one tool of self destruction and death of any race of people who wants to be positive and do what's right in Creation. It now has its own kind of nepotism going on in our communities and neighborhoods.

It's always hostile and abusive to the authority of respect, love, justice and good intentions. It has aided and abetted the rise of disrespect, dishonor, and disunity for decades. It has caused the cracks in the foundation of peace, freedom and unity to turn into crevices.

THE GUN and its evil partners always have a hostile and violent intent and it will never involve promoting peace, freedom and unity. It's now the undisputed world champion of mayhem, disrespect, dishonor and disunity in our communities and neighborhoods. THE GUN is never a metaphor of change and reform in our communities and neighborhoods,

It will never rejuvenate and prepare young people and children to be ready for the battle of good intentions over evil spirits. It now has love, respect and good intentions on shakier ground than five decades ago.

THE GUN and it's a partners are always unconscious when it comes to Creator's original plan which is GOOD WILL CONQUER EVIL AND LOVE WILL TRIUMPH OVER HATE.

Being unconscious is the number one reason THE DRAMA STILL CONTINUES.

THE GUN

THE GUN XI

COMMUNITIES AND NEIGHBORHOODS

By

Dave R. Queeley

THE GUN is the number one reason why We the People cannot live together as one nation working towards a better life in our communities and neighborhoods which are now called Dodge City. It's now despicable and disrespectful to all living things in our communities and neighborhoods, human beings and animals.

Despite the condemnation of THE GUN it still has not stopped young people and children from killing one another on a regular basis in our communities and neighborhoods. It is still the only serial killer that is still at large causing mayhem and havoc in our communities and neighborhoods. It will never let young people and children who own it have a clear perception of the truth, doing what's right and being a positive person living in our communities and neighborhoods.

THE GUN will never have a blue print for peace, freedom and unity for our communities and neighborhoods to follow. It's keeping our communities and neighborhoods on the one track mind and road to self destruction, eternal hell fire and death.

In the 21st century it will never be a humanitarian tool, it always out sources the dirty work to its partner and it always claims to have clean hands in a court of law.

THE GUN has supernatural demonic powers from the unknown and dark side that is destroying the soul of our communities and neighborhoods.

It is now causing a new holocaust in our communities and neighborhoods.

It's now more popular than the Creator's original plan and the Laws of Creation in our communities and neighborhoods and will never bring great blessings and love to our communities and neighborhoods. It will only bring self destruction, misery and death all the time.

THE GUN does not have the eternal power to help resurrect peace, freedom and unity in our communities and neighborhoods. Pulling the trigger of THE GUN will never be a sign of good courage and respect. Pulling the trigger of THE GUN will always remain a sign that its partners are still spiritually and mentally dead to love, justice and good intentions. It now has its partners worshipping a multitude of gods and idols with no end in sight in our communities and neighborhoods.

THE GUN is the tool that will be used to destroy our communities and neighborhoods so that the one world government and one world religion can emerge and take center stage in our communities and neighborhoods as the new way of life without any more mental and spiritual trouble from love, respect and good intentions. It will never try to convey the reassuring message of love, respect and good intentions as the first step to being positive to its partners who are mentally and spiritually dead.

It now has hopelessness, greed, disrespect, dishonor and disunity among the highest and deepest aspirations of young people and children now living in our communities and neighborhoods.

THE GUN is the number one reason why the blood baths continue to be, with blood being drained from the veins of young people and children on the streets of our communities and neighborhoods on a daily basis.

The time has come to put THE GUN on trial for aiding and abetting all those random, senseless and unnecessary shootings and killings that continue to happen in our communities and neighborhoods on a daily basis. THE GUN and its partner will never lead our communities and neighborhoods in the right direction of being positive or to help them in their time of need mentally and spiritually.

It now has the alleged perpetrator of the heinous and violent crimes that are now taking place in our communities and neighborhoods getting younger and younger as the days go by. THE GUN and its partner will soon stick a fork in our communities and neighborhoods because their goose will be cooked.

THE GUN and its partner has turned our communities and neighborhoods into valleys of self destruction, misery and death; where love, justice and good intentions is now like looking for a needle in a hay stack.

The authority of respect, love, justice and good intentions will thwart any attempt by THE GUN and its partner to conquer our communities and neighborhoods.

The time has come for fire to burn THE GUN out of our communities and neighborhoods forever.

THE GUN

GUN PART XII
LEGEND
By
Dave R. Queeley

In the 21st century, the GUN is now a living legend and its partners are either dead or in the pit of doom, injustice and misery (jail or prison)

The GUN has played a crucial role in the decline of the authority of respect, love, justice and good intentions in our communities and neighborhoods.

It's a living legend that has the people, young and old, not remembering Wilmot Edward Blyden and Marcus Garvey. What they stood for has gone out the window of life. Now, it's no more, one God, one aim and one destiny. Just shoot it out, cowboy style.

THE GUN's legacy is complicated but secure because of "NO SNITCHING". It's a code countless people, young and old follow on a daily basis, do or die.

It's a living legend that now has the police department and government unable to quell crime, solve murder cases and lower one of the highest per capita murder rates in the world.

This legacy now has some people, young and old, saying bleep the Nickelodeon image of doing what's right and positive as long as it has something to do with love, respect and good intentions.

The GUN is legendary for keeping the endless cycle of revenge killings and shootings going on in our communities and neighborhoods.

It's a living legend that is trying very hard to solidify, its number one spot as the world's greatest life taker. In the 21st century, it now has outclassed the competition by far.

It's the only tool that emulates hate and disrespect on a daily basis. It's a vulture that only will react to negativity, that's why it remains legendary.

The GUN legacy is a permanent threat against the mental and spiritual stability that is needed in our communities and neighborhoods. The time has come to PUT DOWN THE GUN and to bring back this stability so that truth and honor can shine brightly like a star once again.

It's so legendary that it has some people, young and old, saying in the 21st century, they would rather be in jail, charged by 12 other people a.k.a. jurors than being shot dead and being carried by six to the cemetery, so they always carry a GUN for self protection. Whenever they get caught with the GUN, they always say it's for protection.

It's so legendary that it's showing the world an evil and negative portrayal of our communities and neighborhoods as a very dangerous place to live and visit.

The GUN has gotten so big headed and stubborn that there is no room for compromise anymore. This has affected the way people now treat one another on a daily basis.

It is so legendary that the only time the church pews are filled up is when the family is coming together for a funeral.

This legacy will never be about breathing more life into love, justice and good intentions. It has no passion for seeing these attitudes and actions staying alive in our communities and neighborhoods.

The GUN wants them out of the way, maybe dead, so they can stop interfering with its master's original plan, which is to steal, to divide and to conquer all.

It's so legendary it could use a straight jacket and a couple of Prozac pills to keep it under control.

The GUN is so legendary it now has our younger population disappearing like a magic trick being performed at the circus.

This legacy will never recharge or replace the dying batteries of love, justice and good intentions. That's why it seems like life is a downward spiral, full of mental and spiritual trouble.

The GUN legacy has some people, young and old who keep on attempting or committing mental and spiritual suicide when they pull the trigger of the GUN. They have lost all self control, self-love, self-confidence and self-respect and Evil wins again.

This legacy has some people, young and old dying from their addiction, still in denial and needing psychological help, but continuing to refuse to admit they have a problem.

The GUN legacy has become so legendary for keeping so many people, young and old, at the bottom of the evil barrel of disrespect, dishonor and disunity fighting like crabs to get out.

It has been historically unjust and disrespectful to some people, young and old that they have forgotten about longevity and old age.

In the 21st century it's so legendary that it now has some people, young and old, worshiping it as a supreme being, asking its master for supreme power to continue to be evil and disrespectful every day.

This legacy use to paint a rosy picture that leads to false

expectations, self-destruction and death staying alive in our communities and neighborhoods.

The GUN legacy is not shrinking; it now has reached A list status as a superstar in some people's lives. The time has come for the people, young and old, to separate themselves from being a part of this evil entourage and world.

It's a living legend that has some people, young and old, now thinking and believing that being a part of the recovery of respect, love, justice and good intentions in our communities and neighborhoods that they are now wimps and soft like butter in the sun. And that's not true. It leads to the paradise of truth and honor being established in our communities and neighborhoods that is long, long overdue.

The GUN is a living legend that has some people wanting and calling for federal supervision and protection from being extinct in the future.

This legacy now has some people, young and old, mentally and spiritually lost like Nemo.

THE GUN XIII

PROTEST AGAINST

By

Dave R. Queeley

The time has come for the real protest against gun violence and crime to begin before it's too late for any type of action. We the People are now threatened by the enormous amount of illegal guns that are on the streets of our communities and neighborhoods causing mental and spiritual havoc on a daily basis. When the protest against gun violence and crime begins, it will be the first step in teaching young people and children that the taking of a life by any member of society, cannot and will not be taken lightly anymore. It's time We the People tighten our belts and start protesting every day until things turn around in our communities and neighborhoods. For the criminal element to know the time has come for them to PUT DOWN THE GUN. If you're not a part of the solution then you are a part of the problem. A key step in stopping gun violence and crime will be for the authority of respect, love, justice and good intentions to regain mental and spiritual control back over our communities and neighborhoods.

The time has come to stop letting THE GUN continue its mental and spiritual rampage that is now ruining or communities and neighborhoods future. Hopefully the authority will inspire others to come out and join the protest that needs to be once a month and not just once every six months or once a year. These protests will let the criminal element know We the People are not going to tolerate any more violent crimes and when we see a crime happening we will call the police. It will not be known as snitching but it will be called and known as S.A.V.E., Stepping Against Violence Every time.

The reconstruction of the authority of respect, love, justice and good intentions in our communities and neighborhoods has been painfully slow and it has caused gun violence and crime to rise out of control with no true end in sight. No one in their right mind ever expected the authority of respect, love, justice and good intentions would rise from the rubble of disrespect, dishonor and disunity over night. It will be a long task that will take decades and it will need young people and children to get recommitted to it for the long haul. Everyone is vulnerable in this poisonous atmosphere that our communities and neighborhoods continue to be cloaked in: sadness, misery and always grieving for those who were injured or who have been killed.

THE GUN continues terrorizing our communities and neighborhoods with all those random, senseless and unnecessary killing and shooting sprees that continue to happen in the communities and neighborhoods where love, justice and good intentions has decayed dramatically since 1965, the year we got the right to vote or die. Love, justice and good intentions are teaching young people and children how to start following the Laws of Creation if they want to see true peace and unity happen in this life time. The down fall to peace and unity is greed, hate and selfishness which are off springs of evil.

THE GUN remains a potent threat to the survival of our communities and neighborhoods future. When the protest against gun violence and crime starts it will represent We the People's determination to stop our future from living fast and dying young. The authority of respect, love, justice and good intentions should play a constructive role in the protest as a responsible member and citizen of our communities and neighborhoods. The authority will hopefully help dodge the planned extinction that Satan and his angels of destruction have been working on for decades.

THE GUN will never lead We the People into a gracious and prosperous future. Gun violence and crime has caused a new age and sense of paranoia to grab hold of our communities and neighborhoods and its paralyzing the people with a fear of being robbed, raped and murdered at any time for no good reason at all. In many ways it seems like the end of the era of peace, honor and unity has gone out the window of life never to happen again.

THE GUN will never apologize for causing this to happen. It now has a profound effect on our communities and neighborhoods and on the culture of doing what's right and positive in life. Some people are still frustrated by the long delay of protest against gun violence and crime. When the protest begins it will be a zero tolerance policy, YOU DO THE CRIME YOU DO THE TIME. No more pat on the back sentencing guidelines, do the time will be the consequence, believe it or not. Not joining the protest against gun violence and crime will be a poison pill to all who remain silent. The protest will be important but it will be only one piece of the bigger picture. The protest will mean We the People are really and truly serious about removing this cancer that is growing out of control in our communities and neighborhoods.

We will not leave any part or reminder of this cancer on the landscape of our communities and neighborhoods. It will be a clean sweep. Gun violence and crime is now deeply rooted in hatred, ill will and lust for personal gains and material possession. We the People must never forget THE GUN is not a gift of love, justice and good intentions, it's never consistent. It's always full of the passion of ups and downs that sometimes lead to self destruction, misery and death.

THE GUN now has some people refusing to acknowledge there is a Creator and to seek the truth, which is GOOD WILL CONQUER EVIL AND LOVE WILL TRIUMPH OVER HATE. These spiritually and mentally dead people continue putting their faith, love and respect in THE GUN.

PROTEST EVERY DAY AGAINST THE GUN!

THE GUN PART XIV
STILL HERE
By
Dave R. Queeley

The GUN is still here, in the 21st century, trying it's best to hit our communities and neighborhoods with a death sentence.

It's still here, having some people, young and old, still addicted to the side effects of materialism, disrespect, dishonor and disunity, which are self-destruction and death. Sometimes it seems they will never find the rehab center of truth and honor to seek help.

It's still here, having some people wanting to speak out about it, only on the conditions of anonymity. These people have seemed to forget these attitudes and actions do not help solve the problem; it only helps to make it worse.

The GUN is still here, causing a whole lot of bleeping mental and spiritual danger in the people, young and old lives with no true solution and end in sight. This is one of the main reasons why the decline of love, respect and good intentions continues to happen right in front of their eyes

The GUN is still here, and caused the educational system to have law-enforcement officers working as security officers. Schools are now looking like a juvenile delinquent center. What a shame!

In the 21st century it's still here, still having the people, young and old, not wanting to uphold what's right and positive, which is the Creator's original plan and Laws of Creation, causing some people, young and old, to be emotionally out of control and to go temporarily insane sometimes.

It's still here, stopping the true beginning of the long overdue healing process that we the people need to go through in life so that the paradise of truth and honor can be established soon.

This enemy is still here, having the people, young and old, not strengthening their self bond with the Creator's original plan and Laws of Creation as an everyday activity in life.

The GUN is still here, having some people still living in the cardboard castles of injustice, evil and darkness a.k.a. planned doom thinking and believing they can survive a natural disaster in them.

It's now holding some people in contempt of court and church for not spreading the Creator's original plan all over our communities and neighborhoods and for not following the Laws of Creation to the fullest, until prophecy is fulfilled.

And making sure young people and children do not become lightning rods for truth and honor and they do not to promote or support love, justice and good intentions, staying alive in our communities and neighborhoods.

The GUN is still here, not having the people, young and old taking advantage of the special benefits and immunity that is granted by the Creator, only if they are involved as an individual with love, respect and good intentions helping it to victory over evil for world supremacy

It's still here distracting all cultures, traditions and religions around the world of the rich and poor.

Selling its evil pedigree and no good integrity as the true way of life to being successful and prosperous.

The GUN is still here, hurting and killing children and young people of all economical background and status. It does not differentiate between poor or rich, it's just taking lives, nothing else.

It now has some people feeling worn down and disheartened by all the senseless, random and unnecessary shootings and killings that they still can't find any solution to stopping from continuing to happen like lightning striking.

In the 21st century it's now helping gangs, drug dealers and evil doers to keep on destroying the mental and spiritual tranquility that used to exist in our communities and neighborhoods like back in the good old days of one God, one aim, one destiny.

The GUN is still here, having some people, young and old, lacking the visibility to seeing love, justice and good intentions on the horizon in their lives anytime soon.

It's still here, having some people young and old, still rejecting love, justice and good intentions as their highest and top priority in life for the unusual combinations of hopelessness, materialism, disrespect, dishonor and disunity that continues to reveal not so good statistics showing evil is winning the battle with good for right now in the 21st century.

The GUN is still here, monitoring and spying on the people to see who has a weak mind, body and soul, who are willing and wants to become its partner in life.

These partners keep on forgetting this evil man-made gadget of death and self- destruction comes with no expiration date. It still has some people, young and old, ignoring and continues to disrespect the Creator's original plan and Laws of Creation on a regular basis.

The GUN is still here, having some people, young and old, still lacking internal control, communication and respect for one another or anything that involves doing what's right and positive in life.

It's still here, in the way of some people, young and old, not helping to increase their focus on stopping and finding new crime-fighting ways and tools to stop injustice, evil and darkness a.k.a. planned doom from advancing on love, respect and good intentions territory and conquering it.

It's still alive knowing that it's time as a world leader is running out slowly but surely it will not be used as a tool of protection or destruction anymore. All that will be needed is love, respect and good intentions being practiced on a daily basis.

The GUN is still here, keeping the prison system busy with so much work, they can't hire enough people to do the evil and dirty work as prison guards, going deeper into the 21st century.

The GUN is still here, trying to repeat and reach that illegal target of 62 murders in one year in the Virgin Islands. It continues with its double-digit increase in murders and assaults trying to reach triple digits.

It's still here, having the people, young and old forgetting about the revival of the authority of respect, love, justice and good intentions in their lives. Instead it has them wasting time fighting and killing one another for no godly reason under the sun and moon.

The GUN is still here, free like the Zodiac Killer, always ready to kidnap and kill as many minds, bodies and souls for the angel named Lucifer a.k.a. Satan the devil, who is the originator of unfaithfulness, destruction and the hopelessness that has been filling our communities and neighborhoods cup and now it's running over with body organs and blood.

THE GUN IS STILL HERE!
12-29-2012

THE GUN PART XV
THE TIME HAS COME
By
Dave R. Queeley

The time has come for the people, young and old, to PUT DOWN THE GUN, stop disobeying and disrespecting the Creator's original plan and start following the Laws of Creation, going deeper into the 21st century, so they can wake up with a peace of mind, linked to the Creator all day, every day without any stress from greed.

It's time to dissect the GUN and drain it of its power and life once and for all.

The time has come for the people, young and old, to become numb to the GUN and start the progression to the paradise of truth and honor.

In the 21st century the people, young and old, who are still having an affair with the GUN need to wake up and wise up to the fact that the GUN does not love no one but itself.

It's time for this evil man-made gadget of self-destruction and death to be at the end of the rope of the authority of respect, love, justice and good intentions hanging from a tree.

The time has come for the GUN to stop walking next to the people in the public causing unnecessary tension all day long.

It's time for the conglomerate and bandwagon to go up in smoke like the World Trade Center in New York City.

The people, young and old, have to learn that the GUN will never be anyone's real homey, no matter how hard they try to please it.

In the 21st century these same people have to stop appreciating the GUN more than life, because that's backwards. It's always life before the GUN, self-destruction, and death.

The time has come for the GUN to stop having some of the people, young and old, twisted like dread locks, feeling like with the GUN they can do anything they want to in life.

It's time for the GUN to stop being around, tempting the weak minded to pull the trigger. When and if they do pull the trigger they die inside and has just sold their mind, body, and soul to injustice, evil and darkness for the rest of their lives, living in the pit of doom, injustice and misery, which is now called jail or prison.

It's time to stop the people, young and old, who are hell-bent on destroying themselves with the GUN and that's real talk, **"we have to put it down for real."**

The time has come to stop the GUN from turning our communities and neighborhoods into a scary and dangerous place to live and visit.

The people, young and old, have to finally accept the fact that the GUN has left a lifetime of mental, emotional and spiritual wreckage in its wake.

And it's time for the GUN to RIP meaning rest in peace instead of RIP meaning relaxing in paradise taking lives.

The time has come for the people young and old who are involved with the GUN on an everyday basis to understand, "when karma comes back around. It's always something serious".

Parents must stop letting the GUN become their children and young people's role model they look up to in life.

It's time for the GUN to get out of the people, young and old, pathway of life, so that they can see the potency of the Creator's original plan and Laws of Creation, which is the only exit plan out of the swamp and cesspool of injustice, evil and darkness a.k.a. planned doom that does not lead to self-destruction and death.

The time has come for the unsafe quackery of the GUN to stop being practiced in our communities and neighborhoods. This quackery is causing young people and children to live fast and die young.

In the 21st century, it's time for our communities and neighborhoods to come up with a true plan of attack and the commitment to follow it until they see the destruction of the GUN, so it does not exist anymore in life.

It's time for the people, young and old, to stop engaging in the unlawful and disrespectful behaviors and attitudes that continues to cement the GUN legacy in our communities and neighborhoods.

The time has come to put the genie named the GUN back into its bottle. But some people continue to think it's too damn late for this to happen. It's now out of control.

And it's time to put an end to the GUN'S political belief that now resembles those of Benito Mussolini and Adolf Hitler who promised to revive the economy and to restore pride, respect and hope, but then all of a sudden it was total destruction all around.

The people, young and old, have to start seeking a greater quality of life that is more important than the GUN. This greater quality of life always has to do with love, justice and good intentions, which is superior to all other pathways and lifestyles.

The time has come for the police to start conducting surveillance in our communities and neighborhoods to see where the GUN has been hiding, since it went on the run from being convicted for aiding and abetting all these senseless, random and unnecessary killings and shootings that has been taking place lately in our communities and neighborhoods.

The people, young and old, have to stop surrendering their mind, body and soul to the enemy, which is the GUN and become a warrior of war fighting the darkness of eternity.

The time has come for B.L.A.C.K. Brothers Leading Against Crime and Killings to be the new deliverers of the people, young and old, who remain in mental and spiritual captivity how to turn away from ever picking up the gun. Picking up the gun, a person will never be positive, godly and righteous, no time in life.

It's time for the barbed wire love of the GUN to stop taking place in our communities and neighborhoods

The time has come for the vagabonds and rogues who carry a GUN on a daily basis to always remember "life is too short to continue making silly mistakes every day."

It's time for the authority of love, respect and good intentions to become the new landlord that would evict the evil and destructive tenant named the GUN from our communities and neighborhoods without any police escort.

The time has come for the people, young and old to stop letting F. E. A. R. of the GUN dictate their destiny and future.

F. E. A. R. means False Expectations Appearing in Real.

GUN PART XVI
DISHARMONY
By
Dave R. Queeley

It's time for We the People to look at the track record of the GUN causing disharmony in our communities and neighborhoods for decades. The track record of the lives it has saved is zero, but the track record of the lives it has destroyed is countless.

The GUN and disharmony has aristocratic origins and is distantly related to injustice, evil and darkness a.k.a. planned doom that started 500 years ago when our ancestors first stepped foot off the s/v Jesus Christ onto the land the settlers called the New World.

It has caused some people, young and old, to "don't care" or "give a bleep" if they live or die anymore, going deeper into the 21st century.

This will never give the people, young and old the hope and faith to move on in life from living on the fantasy island of materialism, disrespect, dishonor and disunity that has been keeping them apart for the last couple of decades.

The GUN and disharmony has our communities and neighborhoods sinking deeper and deeper into the abyss of darkness that leads to eternal hell fire and death.

The GUN is always involved with hatred and violence. It now has warfare on a global scale out of control and has turned some people into greedy and self-centered individuals who are only lovers of money, the root of all evil. These attitudes and actions has some people, young and old becoming egotistical individuals who continue stirring up hatred, envy and disrespect for one another every day that the sun rises and the moon sets.

In the 21st century the GUN still has some people, young and old, living in the rainbow land of mental and spiritual economical poverty and darkness because they have lost their self-control, self-love, self-confidence and self-respect for the Creator's original plan and following the Laws of Creation as an everyday activity in life.

It will never help the people, young and old, with the reemergence of respect, love, justice and good intentions happening in our communities and neighborhoods, once again, because it leads to truth and honor being a part of their lives and it will finally let them realize the time has come to PUT IT DOWN.

The GUN and disharmony will never treasure the lives and memories of the people, young and old, that its partner has robbed of their lives. It sometimes feels and seems like our communities and neighborhoods can't catch their breath after all these senseless, random and unnecessary shootings and killings that continue to happen.

Disharmony will never give the people, young and old, the opportunities and potential to change the world back from very bad to very good. It's a responsibility, some people, young and old, are not willing to take on in this lifetime.

The GUN loves being in the lime light and will not give the people, young and old, the courage and strength to stop picking it up and doing something stupid.

The GUN and disharmony don't want the people, young and old, to accept the fact that their noncommittal way of life is preventing them from moving forward to seeing the paradise of truth and honor established in our communities and neighborhoods in the 21st century.

It's the highway or freeway that leads to self destruction and death.

This highway or freeway is always filled bumper to bumper with shining luxury vehicles of evil driving straight into darkness without pressing breaks causing a crash.

The GUN and disharmony keeps the people, young and old, forgetting about the most important and genuine aspect of life, which is to always have respect, love, justice and good intentions in your life as the highest and top priority in life.

It now has some people, young and old, continuing to pretend to be something they are not. Evil doers or murderers, no one in life was ever born evil they were all born in love as a child. They were taught to become evil.

The GUN and disharmony don't like the fact that some people are not afraid to speak out against them all day, every day, even if it means losing their lives.

In the 21st century, the people, young and old continue to forget about their real journey in life, which is to reestablish the paradise of truth and honor that kept our ancestors alive 500 years ago.

The GUN will make sure that the marriage some people have with injustice, evil and darkness will never come to an end.

Disharmony has made some people quit going to church and continue misrepresenting the Creator's original plan and Laws of Creation on a regular basis.

It will always make sure there are no guards at the border, no passports or visas required to enter the gates of eternal hellfire, it will be enter at your own risk.

The GUN and disharmony still has the people slowly creeping down the road of life that does not lead to the authority of love, respect and good intentions, but has them speeding down the road that leads to self destruction and death, like life is a game.

They will not let the people who are mentally and spiritually in captivity shake off the taboo of greed is good, and to make sure they never take the authority of respect, love, justice and good intentions seriously in the 21st century.

The GUN and disharmony will not let these people make inroads in the Civil War of good over evil.

In the 21st century they need to be prosecuted to the fullest extent of the law without any plea deal on the table, so that young people and children can finally see that crime does not pay.

It now has our communities and neighborhoods drowning in a sea of crime and violence that needs to be eradicated now. Otherwise the joy and happiness of life will continue to die slowly.

The GUN and disharmony will never let parents understand the horrors that continue to rip their lives apart wondering why their children and young people like visiting the underground bunker of no return.

In the 21st century, the GUN and disharmony has not been kind to the people, young and old. It continues to tear their lives apart. It now has them falling today with no bottom in sight.

The gun and disharmony have the people, young and old, forgetting that "all good things must come to an end". So it's time these evil feelings, attitudes and actions come to a bleeping end right now with no more disharmony insight.

THE GUN PART XVII
CAUSING
By
Dave R. Queeley

In the 21st century, THE GUN is causing the people, young and old, to forget about the great chemistry they used to have before it was ever invented.

THE GUN is causing the people, young and old, to become selfish, greedy and tremendously evil individuals going deeper into the 21st century. We the People now live in a world where so many people continue to turn away from anything that has to do with love, respect and good intentions.

It has caused some people, young and old, to forget that no situation is hopeless, if We the People work together to contribute positive energies back into the universe.

THE GUN is causing the franchise of injustice, evil and darkness to now open up shops all over our communities and neighborhoods because of some people's common faith in it as their Messiah in the battle of good over evil.

THE GUN is causing the existence of the authority of respect, love, justice and good intentions as an everyday activity in the world to decline to homeless levels, not being worthy of worship anymore.

It has caused the people to remain silent about the rising crime and murder rates, without being outraged about how high it has reached in 21st century.

The evil man-made gadget of self-destruction and death is causing the pace at which young people and children are dying to speed up to over 100 miles per hour, and soon there will be no more young people and children to carry on in the future.

These evil gadgets are causing injustice, evil and darkness a.k.a. planned doomed to become a supernova.

It has caused some people, young and old, to forget to ask themselves this one question, which is not a trick question; "what will I gain if I lose my life?" The answer will always be nothing, because there is no profit in dying.

THE GUN is causing our communities and neighborhoods to be transformed into the new deathtrap zone, where hopelessness, greed, disrespect, dishonor and disunity will continue to run rampantly with no end in sight for miles. If this zone continues, the people, young and old, will never be free of impurities again.

THE GUN is causing the people, young and old, to keep on forgetting that it will never be faithful to anyone. It's always a double crosser and cheater, in its relationship and friendship with its partners.

The people, young and old, who have forgotten about the deceptively simple truth, when love, respect and good intentions reaches out to you in life, it's always a sin if you don't reach back and grab a hold of it.

It has now caused the people and the world to go morally, mentally and spiritually bankrupt and might need a personal stimulus package from the White House to stay afloat and alive for the next five decades.

It is causing the people, young and old, social and communication skills to get poorer and poorer as days go by.

THE GUN is causing some people, young and old, to keep on surrounding themselves with individuals whose only amazing talent is to be evil, hateful and disrespectful to one another on a daily basis.

It now has some people, young and old, continuing to struggle to emerge triumphantly as true survivors of injustice, evil and darkness in the 21st century.

It has caused respect and manners, like saying "Good Morning, Good Afternoon and Good Night" to go out the doors and windows of life going deeper and deeper into the 21st century.

In the 21st century it is still causing the people, young and old, to continue struggling for a real foothold in their adopted homeland of injustice, evil and darkness a.k.a. planned doom, while they are crumbling inside without love, respect and good intentions in their lives on a daily basis.

THE GUN is causing the rotation of love, respect and good intentions to begin to slow down and its gravitational pull to be weakened so that darkness will stretch on forever.

It has caused some people to feel abandoned and lonely if they do not have it on their side at all times.

THE GUN is causing some people to think and feel like they can walk through the fires of injustice, evil and darkness any time they want to without getting burned, if they own one of these man-made gadgets of self-destruction and death.

It's causing its partners to keep on pulling off all kinds of cowardly acts, when they pull the trigger that leads to the pit of doom, misery and injustice.

THE GUN is causing the people, young and old, to have relatives and friends who have been assaulted and murdered by the guns evil partners.

It has caused some people, young and old, not wanting to remain optimistic about the future, because right now the gun is destroying it.

It will always cause the people who are mentally and spiritually dead wanting to seek revenge.

In the 21st century it has caused some people, young and old to forget that everything in life has a beginning and they also have an end. The people who have picked up the gun,   had a start so their end must come: when they choose to PUT IT DOWN and return to spreading the Creator's original plan and following the Laws of Creation. When this happens respect, love, and good intentions will return to its glory days.

THE GUN is causing our law enforcement officers to stop patrolling our communities and neighborhoods on a daily basis. They only come when something serious happens. Back in the good old days, police officers used to be inspirational leaders in our communities and neighborhoods. In the 21st century, some people, young and old, now think and believe some of these officers are just criminals with a badge.

No disrespect to all the good cops who are really protecting and serving the people for real. **Ofc. Roy A. Chesterfield, you big every time. Keep up the good work with The Law and You**. Who feels it knows it.

In the 21st century this evil man-made gadget of self-destruction and death have some people, young and old, continuing to visit the evil place called the Five-Star Hotel Of No Return, which is located 6 feet underground The problems go far beyond the newspaper headlines and tabloid gossip. The problem here is that death is real and it's the real end of the world, not December 21, 2012.

THE GUN is causing so much friendly fire in the battle of good over evil, it's ridiculous. The time has come to publicly strip the gun of its deadly rank.

It's time to get rid of it!

THE GUN PART XVIII
IN THE 21ST CENTURY
By
Dave R. Queeley

In the 21st Century, Mr. Realistic, a.k.a. John the Baptizer intends to present a truthful picture of THE GUN with his writings in his book named, "Put It Down ". So here we go again.

In the 21st century, THE GUN has an insane and outrageous level of crime and violence going on in our communities and neighborhoods which continues to lead to self-destruction and death every single day that goes by.

It's stealing young people and children's innocence and will never give it back once it has it in the bag of injustice, evil and darkness a.k.a. planned doom.

It has some people now feuding with love, respect and good intentions all the time. They are afraid of being hit by the divine spirit of truth and honor, it would help open up their mind, body and soul doing what's right and positive in life and to stop them from being evil monsters of darkness.

The fact is, the law says it's illegal to sell, to carry and to own a gun, but the reality is there are lots of lawbreakers in our communities and neighborhoods causing mental and spiritual tension and havoc just because they have access to a gun.

In the 21st century, there aren't enough Band-Aids to cover all the bullet holes that THE GUN has put into our communities and neighborhoods lately.

It's the new Caligula, who was the Emperor of Destruction and Mayhem in Roman times.

In our communities and neighborhoods, there are a few evil and poisonous people who continue to bring in large quantities of drugs, guns and military style assault weapons that are never needed in our communities and neighborhoods for no good or godly reason under the sun.

THE GUN has trusted some people, young and old, into the messy lifestyle and negative pathways of greed that is ruining their reputations as truth seekers.

In the 21st century, the imaginative world of THE GUN is now enlightening some people, young and old, on how to be evil doers and murderers of truth and honor. They will never breathe new life into the authority of respect, love, justice and good intentions at any time in life.

It now has some people, young and old, not wanting to become deeply religious and sincere anymore. They have forgotten these attitudes, feelings and actions are the first step to becoming a positive, successful and prosperous person in life.

They have to always remember, as day gives way to night, the Creator is calling out to the people, young and old, to put down the gun because life is too short to be playing with it

In the 21st century, THE GUN is causing some people, young and old, sell out their lives and become disciples and members of one of the angel named Lucifer, secret societies of injustice evil and darkness that has them on a wild goose chase.

It now has the people, young and old, not willing to care to give respect, to get respect back, just because they own a gun.

THE GUN has some people, young and old trading their minds, body and soul for prosperity and success aka getting money.

In the 21st century it continues to lead young people and children down the evil pathways that leads to self-destruction and death

In the 21st century, THE GUN is a nightmare that is a reminder of all the people we have lost senselessly, randomly and unnecessarily. Something has to be done to stop this madness from continuing to happen.

It will never offer condolences to anyone its partner has assaulted and killed. It's always good riddance for being involved because that's its job, to take lives and to respect no one.

In the 21st century, hatred, miscommunication and disharmony are stopping the people from reuniting with the authority of respect, love, justice and good intentions, keeping them further and further apart from the Creators original plan and Laws of Creation as their top and highest priority in their lives.

It has some people, young and old, unprepared mentally and spiritually to handle the difficulties and rigors of war.

The false idol named THE GUN has to be replaced by the real Messiah, which is deep inside all human beings, its love justice and good intentions. These attitudes, feelings and actions will be the fires that will help melt down the guns iron grip on the people's body, mind and soul.

In the 21st century, THE GUN has some people going to the bar to have a few drinks to numb and to help them cope with all the mental and spiritual pain, tension and havoc it continues to cause on a regular basis in our communities and neighborhoods.

THE GUN is now like a skunk, something to beware of at all times. In the 21st century, it's the new drill master of Satan's army of injustice, evil and darkness a.k.a. planned doom

It now has young people and children mental and spiritual state getting worse and going down the drain as the days go by. These adolescents and preteens were not taught by their parents that without self-control, self-love, self-confidence and self-respect the evil spirit that comes with picking up or owning a gun will always control you.

In the 21st century, the man who was the inventor of THE GUN should go down in the Guinness Book of World Records as the man who created the world's most dangerous man-made killer of human beings.

THE GUN has some people, young and old, not wanting to self surrender to the will of the Creator who is love at all times and never hate.

We the People have to set a date for when the long overdue and great discussions about finding solutions and how we are going to solve this major problem, WHICH IS THE GUN..

In the 21st century, THE GUN has some people, young and old, emotionally unstable and thinking that living in the Lala Land of greed, disrespect, dishonor and disunity, they can get rich. Like Buju Banton says, "you see the glamour and the glitter, so you think it's a better road", of life going deeper into the century.

THE GUN PART IXX
DISHARMONY 2
By
Dave R. Queeley

In the 21st century, it's time We the People regain the upper hand and reunite ourselves under the strong monarchy of love, respect and good intentions. This period of life will be known as the great change, reform, improvement to society and the downfall of THE GUN and disharmony.

With THE GUN and disharmony has young people and children keeps on forgetting no one has ever gone and returned from THE FIVE-STAR HOTEL OF DEATH which is located 6 feet underground, "saying how good room service and the food was."

THE GUN have some people, young and old, thinking and saying the best witness to a crime are the ones in the funeral parlor.

Disharmony has some people, young and old, trying to put in an express lane on the highway and freeway that leads to self-destruction and death, so they can get to eternal hellfire faster than ever before.

In the 21st century, THE GUN and disharmony have people forgetting about the Reel Team. The Reel Team is all about loyalty and dedication to seeing good over evil all the time. T. E. A. M. is supposed to mean in the 21st century, Together Everyone Achieves More. This cannot happen with the gun and disharmony.

They are the number one reason why there is a significant increase in violent crimes every year.

In the 21st century, there are some people, young and old, acting like the world revolves around them. These attitudes and actions keep these people struggling with a mental health diagnoses they do not know they have or how to cure it.

THE GUN and disharmony continues to have some people, young and old, keep on falling into all sorts of temptations and traps that keeps love, justice and good intentions disintegrating out of their lives every day, going deeper into the century.

Disharmony is the great expansion of injustice, evil and darkness that keeps the angel named Lucifer a.k.a. Satan the devil royal and evil powers of alive. Dignity and respect will never be a part of the equation of life.

THE GUN now has some people, young and old, not having any mental and spiritual awareness about the Creator's original plan of how to follow the Laws of Creation until the end of time. These people think and believe the plan and laws of life are not needed as long as they have a gun.

In the 21st century, THE GUN and disharmony is so diabolical, they have some people, young and old lives in a downward spiral that leads to self-destruction and death. These places do not spell out success and prosperity at any time in life.

They continue to create an atmosphere of social, mental and spiritual chaos on a daily basis, going deeper into the century with no end in sight.

Disharmony will never help with restoring creation and humanity to the conditions that the Creator originally planned and intended for all people to enjoy with the motto of "**GOOD OVER EVIL ALL THE TIME**".

THE GUN has some people, young and old, not doing the work that is meaningful and satisfying to establish the paradise of truth and honor that will help with the future security, success and prosperity for all.

In the 21st century, THE GUN and disharmony has We the People forgetting it's our duty and responsibility to keep respect, love, justice and good intentions alive. We can't run from it anymore because everyone living came from this point at one time in life before they chose to become evil doers and murderers of truth and honor.

They keep on forgetting these attitudes and actions leave you feeling empty inside and only love, justice and good intentions can fill that empty space and keep them from continuing down the dead end road of injustice, evil and darkness aka planned doom.

Disharmony now has a new mental and spiritual gap emerging between parents and their young people and children going deeper and deeper into the century with no solution or plan to stopping this gap.

THE GUN has some people, young and old, keep on forgetting life is what you make it and it's too short to be playing with it like it's a game.

THE GUN and disharmony has the perception as the Untouchables because they now have the stakes of life higher than they have ever been before.

In the 21st century as long as love, respect and good intentions stay woven into the fabric of our society, We the People will always be around fighting to dethrone THE GUN and disharmony reign as King.

THE GUN and disharmony has some people, young and old, keep on forgetting all human beings were born free and equal. It's their job in life to live united and free of the burdens of "Greed is good."

Disharmony will not let the people, young and old, take on a more assertive role in finding true solutions to the trifling situation that gun violence and crime continues to cause in our communities and neighborhoods.

THE GUN has some people thinking and believing that some young people and children come from the womb violent and evil, but that's a lie. They were created and born in love and taught to become violent and evil.

In the 21st century, THE GUN and disharmony have some people, young and old, living in mental and spiritual squalor, caring about nothing in life that is good and positive.

They are constantly harassing and imprisoning young people and children from the cradle to grave.

We the People have to understand that THE GUN and disharmony is an unattractive alternative to the Creator's original plan and Laws of Creation being followed on a daily basis

In the 21st century, THE GUN and disharmony will never be a divine blessing from the Creator!

THE GUN PART XX
RAPID FIRE: THE ASSAULT RIFLE
By
Dave R. Queeley

"NO ONE KNOWS WHO INVENTED THE GUN, SO if SOMEONE KNOWS PLEASE LET SOCIETY KNOW NOW!"

Weapons of war such as AK-47, AR 15 and M-16 are assault rifles that do not belong in the hands of civilians claiming to be gangsters, the time has come for the renewal of the ban on these types of weapons being on the streets of our communities and neighborhoods. The call for change and reform has fallen on deaf ears, and has always been followed by little or no legislative action at all; the time has really come for We the People to start standing up and speaking out for stricter enforcement of the gun laws that are already on the books. If we can't enforce them, why are they on the books?

Society must remember the attraction between young people and the assault rifle is electric. They seem to can't resist them at all; the assault rifles belong in the hands of soldiers of war and not in the hands of criminals and our children. They belong on the battlefield of war and not on the streets of our communities and neighborhoods. Assault rifles are instruments of evil and destruction with the sole purpose of killing people. The assault rifles presence in our communities and neighborhoods has made life harder, and damn near unbearable. Every night you hear automatic weapons being fired in the air for no good reason at all. All they're doing is disturbing the peace!

The assault rifle has caused gun violence, homicide and crime rates to go through the roof. This is a serious problem that needs to be discussed daily until solutions are explored or found. The assault rifle is now public enemy number one, anyone who owns one has no value and respect for life in the slightest degree. The assault rifle, not only has gun violence and crime on the rise, but it now has it out of control. They have dramatically deteriorated the authority of respect, love, justice and good intentions in our communities and neighborhoods. This is a major problem for society moving forward deeper into the 21st century. We the People must never forget there is no real coordination to restoring confidence in this authority to regain the upper hand in its rivalry with greed, disrespect, dishonor and disunity.

Premature death and long imprisonment are the results of owning an assault rifle. The assault rifle has become some young people's Rock of Gibraltar that they now worship every day with the evil motto of "kill or be killed." It has the homicide and crime rate continuing to soar to unbelievable levels with no serious end in sight. Some people now believe and think we need FBI or CIA intervention to stopping the madness from ripping the life out of our communities and neighborhoods. We the People have to start saturating our crime infested areas of our communities and neighborhoods with law abiding police officers and COPS a.k.a. Citizens On Patrol, with the motto SAVE aka Standing Against Violence Every time. Only then owning an assault rifle, gun violence and crime will decline dramatically.

The assault rifle can fire many bullets quickly with a single pull of the trigger. In the 21st century, it's now an affordable luxury of destruction that now has some young people feeling and thinking like they can live underground and be successful in life. This fiction is not good or positive news for their survival. Society has to admit to themselves that these attitudes and actions are major problems to our future generation staying alive, going deeper and deeper into the 21st century. Peace, freedom and unity cannot be achieved or become a successful act through the barrel of an assault rifle. It's like we're now living back in the wild, Wild West days when life did not mean anything.

The assault rifle has infiltrated our communities and neighborhoods, and now has turned them into one of the sorriest and violent places to live and visit because innocent bystanders are being killed or wounded for no good reason at all. The time has come for society to join operation stop the criminal element. This operation will be very energetic and will not let up until they are all locked away or decide to reform themselves from evil back to having good intentions for one another. The assault rifle has the people who have a twisted mind and are mentally and spiritually dead continuing to chop down one another, like a lawnmower cutting grass.

Evil, injustice and darkness have blinded their minds to good intentions and will never fix or restore their sight, because they have sold their soul, mind and body to evil, injustice and darkness. The people who own an assault rifle are haters of mankind and prisoners of their own consciousness and will it not let them play by the rules of society anytime soon. Lately the assault rifle has been used or believed to have been used in several recent violent crimes that took place in our communities and neighborhoods. In the 21st century young people are now harboring a known fugitive and that is the assault rifle. The legacy of the assault rifle helping kill hundreds of young people will be very hard and impossible to erase. It's now an uninvited guest that is continuing to wreak havoc on our communities and neighborhoods with no true end in sight. It's time to pull aside the veil of secrecy surrounding this uninvited guest.

These uninvited guests can only continue to arrive in our communities and neighborhoods by air or sea. So the smuggling of the ammunitions, drugs and weapons across our borders on a daily basis is the number one reason why there are so many assault rifles in our communities and neighborhoods. The large cachets of ammunition, drugs and weapons that are being moved across our borders and sold on the streets are not street dealers. Street dealers don't have the connections needed and the money it will cost to pay off the people who will look the other way and let them keep coming in. That means Homeland or Border Security are not doing a good job and someone needs to get fired. The people who are getting paid in full to look the other way should always remember, mentally and spiritually dead and unbalanced people should never own a weapon at any time in life, because it's only a recipe for disaster in the future.

In the 21st century, some people now think and believe there are more assault rifles and illegal weapons in our communities and neighborhoods than cars on the streets. The assault rifle, greed, disrespect, dishonor and disunity still continue to have young people trapped and chained down in the evil and dark world of injustice and planned doom. Every day, one of them becomes another statistic, some die or some are in jail for life. All because they own one of these dangerous weapons called an assault rifle. It's now the greatest harlot that continues to lead young people astray from the Creators original plan and Laws of Creation being followed on a daily basis in our communities and neighborhoods.

The time has come for We the People to start severely restricting ownership of these weapons of war. The time has come to start the countdown to ending the assault rifles, reign as King in our communities and neighborhoods and start saving lives, mentally and spiritually. It's time for law and order to be restored now.

PUT THE WEAPONS OF WAR DOWN. WE DON'T NEED THEM IN THIS LIFETIME!

GUN VIOLENCE AND CRIME

By
Dave R. Queeley

Gun violence and crime cannot silence the truth, the truth is always mighty. Gun violence and crime could be brought down by massive public outrage and demonstrations every day. Not once in a while, but every day. Our communities and neighborhoods cannot continue fighting gun violence and crime with a dull knife of defense that has put young and old people's lives in jeopardy. It's time for taking drastic measures and steps to defeating gun violence and crime.

We the People are in the midst of an epidemic, one that threatens the well-being of young people's and children's future. Tackling gun violence or crime and overcoming it will require lots of time, planning and hard work. Returning to having respect, love, justice and good intentions will be the best weapon in our arsenal to stop the epidemic that is now taking place in our communities and neighborhoods. Gun violence and crime has forever stained our society with blood and body organs of young people who have been murdered (62 of them in 2010, the deadliest year on record).

Gun violence and crime are lights that continue to brighten up our communities and neighborhoods while their intentions continue to be darkened by greed and selfishness. Gun violence and crime are now acceptable behaviors in our communities and neighborhoods because on October 29, 2010, they got a slap in the face or true reminder that "if you're poor without money, you don't collect $200 and stay out of jail." The acquittal of the ATF agent, a cold blooded murder, and there was no public outcry, protest and march against this total disrespect and injustice. Here is the reality, if you are a close friend or a family member of the people in charge, you can get away with anything, even first-degree murder.

There are only two ways illegal weapons, bullets and drugs can enter into our society, it's either by air or sea. So it looks like border protection is failing miserably, because gun violence and crime are now at an all-time high. The police now need to find out how and where criminals are getting these illegal weapons, bullets and drugs from. Gun violence and crime continues burning holes into the social fabric of our communities and neighborhoods and our politicians and high-ranking government officials continue to do nothing about this problem. Gun violence and crime now have our communities and neighborhoods living in fear of being robbed or shot, and they are now hesitant to admit it because no one is stressing the importance of communities and neighborhoods working together to find true solutions for gun violence, crime, and all other social ills that continue to affect life in our communities and neighborhoods.

Gun violence, drug abuse and crime are something society has failed to tame and it has altered the way people treat one another in public. The process of change and having respect, love, justice and good intentions is moving on in the right direction, in spite of all the difficulties it now faces with gun violence and crime. The impact of gun violence and crime has been far greater and far worse than society has anticipated and it has now established the fact that the wild, wild West rules will continue to prevail. Some people will claim peace, freedom and unity is now impossible, because the basic obstacle and barrier to peace, freedom and unity is now gun violence, drugs and crime.

These days, we are constantly reminded by the unspeakable acts of gun violence and crime and the damage it continues to inflict upon our communities and neighborhoods. Some people are now fighting against gun violence, drugs and crime because they are "sick and tired of being sick and tired" and they don't want it to become a permanent part of life in the future. Anyone fighting against gun violence, drugs and crime needs a megaphone to get their point across that these things will not be tolerated anymore.

Down with gun violence, drugs and crime. And up with having respect, love, justice and good intentions, the keys to peace, freedom and unity.

END GUN VIOLENCE AND CRIME NOW, BECAUSE THE PEN IS MIGHTIER THAN THE SWORD OR GUN!

GUN VIOLENCE AND CRIME II

By

Dave R. Queeley

"NO MORE BAD PUBLICITY"

It's time for gun violence and crime to pack up and leave our communities and neighborhoods ASAP. We the People now have a mile wide and 6 inch deep problem. It's called gun violence and crime. It's time to battle the ongoing gun violence and crime wave that continues at the demise of our young people's lives and destroying our communities and neighborhoods financially. Gun violence and crime has triggered the breakdown of the social fabric of our communities and neighborhoods and has made an already vulnerable population even more desperate to find solutions to this major problem.

The gun violence and crime phenomenon comes at a time when our communities and neighborhoods are struggling to rebuild having respect, love, justice and good intentions as their highest priority in life. There are hundreds of old and young people still living in mental and spiritual squalor. They continue to see the avalanche of disrespect, dishonor and disunity that is now taking place in their homeland or town getting worse. It's a concern for all of us to do what we can to stop gun violence and crime.

This new phenomenon is the darkest period in our history as people of love, justice and good intentions as their highest priority life. Gun violence and crime is not only a terrible tragedy in our communities and neighborhoods, it's now a global tragedy happening every other second worldwide. Gun violence and crime has grown to epidemic heights with no end in sight. The gun violence and crimes now taking place in our communities and neighborhoods has turned them into an absolute abyss of pain, fear and suffering, sometimes mentally and spiritually. Gun violence and crime now have our communities and neighborhoods bursting at the seams, and no one knows when it will explode into an all out civil war.

Today's law abiding citizen wants their communities and neighborhoods back and want them to once again become a safe place to live and visit. They must realize once the crime-ridden areas of our communities and neighborhoods are contained there will have to be a significant return to having respect, love, justice and good intentions as their highest priority in life so that these crime-ridden areas don't return to being a problem for society anymore. There can be no more excuses for why the gun violence and crime rate is so high.

The perpetrators of gun violence and crimes must be brought to justice and punished to the full weight of the law, no more slap on the wrist or pat on the back sentences. "You do the crime, violent or not, you do a long time in the pit of doom, injustice and misery aka jail or prison." This needs to be society's new motto and message to all young people and children. FOR REAL. It's time society take a firmer stance against gun violence, crime and any other obstacles that continue to hold us back from uniting once and for all in the battle of "Good Intentions over Evil". We the People have to move forward aggressively exploring all our options because our law enforcement authorities are now struggling to curb the spiraling gun violence and crime problem, to no avail.

All communities and neighborhoods need better crime-fighting strategies and methods that will work. Like one: upholding all curfews; two: teaching crime prevention in all schools, churches and homes; and three: provide better job opportunities, only then We the People will see significant reductions in gun violence and crime. In the 21st Century, some people are now venting their frustration privately about gun violence, crime and how badly our government system is handling this crisis we are now facing day and night with automatic gunfire. Gun violence and crime was once rare like a pink diamond in our communities and neighborhoods, but now they have become an every other day event. If society wants to stop gun violence and crime, they need to start giving out books in the trouble areas of our communities and neighborhoods and on the street corners where drugs are sold and watch young people run away like cockroaches do when you turn on the light.

They have forgotten that reading is a fundamental part of life, not gun violence, drugs and crime. They are misled to a phony part of life. In the 21st century, the people in charge continued efforts to pacify or use band aids on the problem of gun violence and crime with no true commitment to finding a solution that will work. One long-term solution is We the People need better and stronger illegal weapons control laws. It's time for We the People to instigate a serious dialogue with the people in charge about how they are going to save our schools, communities and neighborhoods from injustice, drugs, gun violence and crime, before it's too late for any type of action. The inability of the people in charge of government has placed an impossible burden on We the People's backs to solve this major problem.

We the People Have to get really involved and promote or sponsor the changes and reforms that are now needed to improve the quality of life in our communities and neighborhoods. Improving the quality of life for all people will be the first step in stopping gun violence and crime. Poverty breeds all kinds of crimes. It's hard to keep up with the dizzying barrage of reports of crimes involving the use of an illegal weapon. The truth is, gun violence and crime has been happening for decades because the people in charge or in high places used to sweep it under the rug. So no one would notice that we had a problem.

Gun violence and crime will never treat society humanely. The only treatment society will get will always be carnage, bloodshed and death. Gun violence and crime is not affiliated or associated with anything that has good intentions behind it. Gun violence and crime has a longtime collaboration with Satan and his angels of destruction, to steal, to divide and conquer as much souls as they can for him. It's now a plague without a cure. If gun violence and crime continues, our communities and neighborhoods will be insolvent in a few years to come.

Gun violence and crime cannot be changed or reformed overnight, because it took years for things to get so damn bad. And if it continues, there will be martial law, coming soon. Everything and everyone will be on lockdown. The reality is, if any efforts or plans to end the gun violence and crime crisis are likely to take place, it will take decades to be successful, because there are so many illegal weapons and ammunition on the streets of our communities and neighborhoods. Gun violence, drugs and crime continues to be the death of our future generation. Young people and children have forgotten that gun violence, drugs and crime are all part of the devil's workshop, that leads to a lifetime in the pit of doom, injustice and misery aka jail or prison.

It's time for society to do more to contribute to peace, stability and unity because all the unnecessary, senseless and random shootings and killings have brought society one step closer to the brink of an all out civil war. If something isn't done very soon to stop the flow of illegal weapons, ammunition and drugs on the streets of our communities and neighborhoods. Some people say its Arabs, the ones who own the big supermarkets and grocery stores or the Anglo-Saxons who live on the boats. But no one really knows who brings them in.

One thing some people know is, it is politicians, high-ranking government officials and police officers job to find out where the real source is located , before it's too damn late to stop the bloodshed from happening anymore. One or two marches and speeches every six months is not going to solve all the mental and spiritual problems that gun violence and crime causes. It will take maybe one every week, but for sure is needed every month to remind criminals and gangs that We the People are not going to tolerate this madness of random, senseless and unnecessary killings and shootings in our communities and neighborhoods.

This message of gun violence and crime is a call for action. It's time to drain the swamp and cesspool of injustice, evil and darkness a.k.a. planned doom. Our communities and neighborhoods must realize gun violence and crime is an expensive headache, We the People cannot afford and don't need in our life anymore.

GUN VIOLENCE AND CRIME.

GUN VIOLENCE AND CRIME III
START COMPLAINING
By
Dave R. Queeley

Time to lay the facts out on the table for all eyes to see. This action is long overdue. It's time to stop playing around when it comes to stopping or solving the problem of gun violence and crime. The Virgin Islands is a much less harmonious, loving and respectable place, like back in the 60s, 70s and early 80s, when everyone had respect, love, justice and good intentions on their mind, and it was their highest priority in life. Now it's all about getting paid and having money, being selfish and greedy and letting disrespect, dishonor and disunity continue to control their lives.

There is now no more respect and love, it died decades ago when drugs, gun violence and crime took over the communities and neighborhoods. Gun violence and crime will continue to be on the rise as our economy worsens because of out dated principles by politicians and high-ranking government officials who have no remedies for our mental, economical and spiritual problems We the People have to live with every day. We need viable alternatives that work and will solve all those problems, We the People have to live with every day. It's time for them to back up all those empty words and promises with actions. It's time for society to start complaining and for it to escalate to the highest peak of any mountain around the world so that the people in charge can hear and understand, We the People are not going to take any more BS or sit back and continue to be robbed in the name of God for the In God We Trust, which is the dollar bill.

Complaining means to express grief, pain or discontent and to make a formal accusation or charge. Complaining will never be reeling from a backlash and be blackballed, because out of darkness came light. There'll never be darkness coming out of light. Light brings forth more light. Complaining will not stop until the people in charge have come up with real and practical plans and solutions to help the people who are suffering from hearing automatic gunfire night after night in their communities and neighborhoods. Gun violence and crime has taken a huge financial and human toll on our communities and neighborhoods. Back in the good old days of having respect, love, justice and good intentions, it had an old saying, "nothing good ever happens after dark". It was always all in the in the night that violence broke out. Now in the 21st century it's happening early in the morning, late afternoon or night, and anyplace now, even in the hospital and at funerals.

These demented acts were the straw that broke the camel's back and it took the cake for some people. They are now on the side of complaining and think something needs to be done immediately about stopping gun violence and crime. They are now the new Jim Crow of the 21st century and they now have our communities and neighborhoods in turmoil. There'll be no end to gun violence and crime until the criminal element can no longer operate freely in the public and cause havoc. We the People must remember Crime stoppers and Neighborhood Watch programs will help in the decline of gun violence and crime, if they come together and work with these programs. It will not be snitching, it will be the first step in restoring law and order in our communities and neighborhoods, turning them back into a real secure and safe place to visit and live without fear of being robbed, raped and murdered for no good reason at all.

The continued violence is a reminder that something needs to be done fast, because the criminal element now have a sanctuary and it's now called "No Snitching". This is a major problem to stopping gun violence and crime in the 21st century. Stopping gun violence and crime will be a titanic struggle because there are so many illegal weapons and ammunition on the streets of our communities and neighborhoods, and it has changed the mental and spiritual landscape in some young people's minds. They have forgotten, you can replace material things, but you cannot replace people's lives once they have died.

They are now living in a new era of no dignity and disrespect which continues to lead them to being morally bankrupt. Gun violence and crime continues to leave our communities and neighborhoods sputtering to stay alive. Gun violence and crime now have our communities and neighborhoods swinging from the chandelier of injustice and disunity. The rising murder and crime rates have put a real dent in whatever little confidence We the People had left in our government system to find solutions to this major problem.

Most of the perpetrators of gun violence and crime are minors, who are behaving like adults and committing all these unnecessary, random and senseless violent crimes. It is tarnishing the image of the Virgin Islands as paradise and a safe place to live and visit. The fear and stress of being a victim of gun violence and crime has now taken over and it's spreading quickly throughout our communities and neighborhoods. This fear now has our communities and neighborhoods under a lot of stress, and it has a lot to do with the rising murder and crime rates. We the People now have to be like the middle east peace broker aimed at lowering the fear and stress level. If it's not lowered, the consequences will continue to be disastrous.

The actions we take in the 21st century will ensure the matter of gun violence and crime is addressed in a manner of consistency, not just lip service anymore, which remains ineffective. The relationship We the People renew in the 21st century towards the progress in the common pursuit of stopping gun violence and crime from continuing to destroy our communities and neighborhoods. The demented acts of violence that We the People continue to read about in the newspaper, hear about on the radio and shown on the TV, should inspire all of us to stand up and start complaining, and not just for a little while. "Saying enough is enough and we are not going to tolerate any more disrespect, dishonor and disunity from anyone living in our communities and neighborhoods".

It's time to fight the mental and spiritual madness now taking place and to campaign against the use of illegal weapons to commit a violent crime and assault. Gun violence and crime continues to be bloody and have body organs spilled on the streets of our communities and neighborhoods, like never seen before. There is now a gulf of indifference between stopping the madness and making them safe so people can live without the fear and stress of being robbed, raped and shot to death for no good reason under the sun and moon at all. Gun violence and crime continues to cause monumental pain and suffering for the people now living in our communities and neighborhoods. We the Peoples main problem right now is that too many people are only complaining about gun violence and crime in the closet, because of fear of losing their jobs. So they will only speak out on the condition of anonymity for fear of retaliation. But they have forgotten, no politicians and high-ranking officials have pledged real improvements in the true solution to stopping the rise of gun violence and crime, which has injured hundreds of young and old people and have killed numerous others over the last five decades.

Men, women and children have been gunned down and assaulted for being in the wrong place at the wrong time. Gun violence and crime are at a disastrous level right now, and it now can be called a crisis, because stopping it from happening is easier said than done. Having respect, love, justice and good intentions has declined significantly in some young and old people's lives. The slow public response to returning to having respect, love, justice and good intentions will continue to cost lives to be lost.

If gun violence and crime continues, We the People will find ourselves in a situation that will not be survivable. A simple message needs to be sent to the next generation of young and old people. This simple message will be, "nothing good comes out of gun violence and crime. So leave the automatic weapons were they belong. In the stores in the USA and not in the Virgin Islands." It's time for gun violence and crime to be ousted.

ACTION SPEAKS LOUDER THAN WORDS. START COMPLAINING NOW!

GUN VIOLENCE AND CRIME IV
MEMORIAL DAY
By
Dave R. Queeley

Everyday should be called Memorial Day in our communities and neighborhoods, because young people and children continue to lose their lives carelessly in the mental, economical and spiritual wars now taking place in our communities and neighborhoods. Gun violence and crime is now a category five pain in the ass for some people, and it's very difficult to come up with real explanations, other than there has not been any commitment or the will to change and seek reform on the part of the people now in charge. These actions continue to put young people and children who are living in our communities and neighborhoods in unnecessary danger. Lack of accountability is one of the core reasons why young people and children are dying like soldiers of war. That's why every day needs to be called Memorial Day.

They have forgotten no one will remember they were an original gangster or whatever the new slang is for boss player. Gun violence and crime is the new Pandora's Box and We the People will never be able to close it again. It has created a very unholy and unhealthy recipe for disaster and self-destruction that is now happening in our communities and neighborhoods. Our communities and neighborhoods are now visibly struggling to maintain composure during these serious times of gun violence and crime that is on the rise constantly. It saddens and shocks some people that our communities and neighborhoods have allowed gun violence and crime to continue to spiral out of control with no end or true solution in sight.

Gun violence and crime represents the ultimate betrayal of love, justice and good intentions in our communities and neighborhoods. Love, justice and good intentions was supposed to protect our communities and neighborhoods, but instead, gun violence and crime has caused some people to lose trust and interest in the mission of good over evil, and it has turned them into savages,(the ones who are spiritually and mentally dead). In the 21st century, they now want a movie or Hollywood style kind of life. Just like Scarface and the results of that lifestyle is always disheartening. That's why every day in our communities and neighborhoods can be called Memorial Day.

Our communities and neighborhoods now need corrective and preventive measures before it's too late for any actions. It's time for our so-called politicians and high-ranking government officials to start funding programs and activities that will steer the mentally and spiritually dead young people and children who are at risk away from gun violence and crime, and from spending a lifetime in the pit of doom and injustice (jail or prison). In the 21st century, politicians and our high-ranking government officials are now mentally, morally and spiritually bankrupt or dead, when it comes to doing what's right for the people who are suffering and being oppressed by gun violence and crime. They are now slumlords and instruments of injustice, evil and darkness aka planned doom. They have forgotten the time has come for stopping the bloodshed and to spare our communities and neighborhoods from any further deterioration of their soul.

Gun violence and crime are now starting to affect the quality of life in our communities and neighborhoods from being America's Paradise to now Nightmare on Elm Street. The criminal element is getting bolder and bolder every day and it's a shame to know that mahogany people are killing each other over simple material things, getting worse with no real solution in sight. Gun violence and crime continues to have some people fearful of leaving their homes at any time of the day for fear of being robbed, raped or murdered for no good reason at all under the sun or moon. Community and neighborhood involvement and services will be more effective in combating gun violence and crime. More iron bars or gated communities and neighborhoods would lead to more separation of the people.

We the People have to start imposing curfews on all underage people being out all times of the night causing havoc. Some people will not mind living under curfew conditions, if it is going to make their communities and neighborhoods a safer place to live and visit. Gun violence and crime continues to have our communities and neighborhoods swinging from the chandeliers of injustice, evil and darkness a.k.a. planned doom. The crippling cost of gun violence and crime has become clearer by the day. Every time you read a newspaper, turn on the radio and TV, all you see and hear about is another random senseless and unnecessary murder and assault.

We the People need to be more aware of the extreme significance and urgency of the task of stopping gun violence and crime, which is now more than necessary. It seems to some people, the authorities have not realized that the situation is getting really serious and needs to be dealt with right away. Gun violence and crime have some people feeling like a second-class citizen in their own homeland, because the new illegal immigrants are now the weapons, drugs and ammunition running wild in the streets of our communities and neighborhoods, causing havoc. It's time to crack down on these illegal immigrants from being on the streets, causing stress and fear of being a victim of a violent crime. They now have some people afraid to go outside by themselves, and it has others wanting to hire private bodyguards to escort them 24 hours, seven days of the week, from their homes until the threat of being robbed, raped or murdered subsides.

Gun violence and crime is now larger than a good education and Satan and his angels of destruction are proud and happy about this happening in the 21st century, because that's their department, to steal, to divide and to conquer as many souls that are needed to help them in the battle with good intentions for world supremacy. They are dancing every night in hell when someone commits a random, senseless and unnecessary murder or assault. It's time for life in our communities and neighborhoods to be , uninterrupted by gun violence and crime, like back in the good old days of having respect, love, justice and good intentions for all.

Gun violence and crime do not provide a lifeline to unity. The only lifeline they provide is death or a lifetime in the pit of doom and injustice. Being a part of gun violence and crime is now a desirable lifestyle some young people and children seek. They now have no interest in doing what's right, like having respect, love, justice and good intentions on their minds and in their lives on a daily basis. It will stop anymore days from being called Memorial Day in our communities and neighborhoods. If gun violence and crime continues, our communities and neighborhoods will be on the edge of mental, economical and spiritual darkness.

We the People have gone too far away from the Creator's original plan and Laws of Creation, and that's a major reason why our communities and neighborhoods are on the edge of darkness. Satan and his angels of destruction now have a hand in running the land. He will never be able to run Creation. Creation is light and he has nothing to do with light, only darkness. That is why he's running the land and not Creation.

NO MAN KNOWETH THE MINUTE NOR THE HOUR, WHEN THE FIRSTBORN OF CREATION WILL COME BACK TO SAVE MANKIND FROM THE SELF-DESTRUCTION OF GUN VIOLENCE AND CRIME.

HAPPY MEMORIAL DAY

GUN VIOLENCE AND CRIME V
CONSEQUENCES
By
Mr. Dave R. Queeley

There is no reason, excuse or explanation to why it's a widespread desire of young people and children to want to carry a gun or dangerous weapon for their so-called protection. A large percentage of young people and children now lack the proper understanding and discipline about the consequences of these actions. It's time to address this problem at the scale that is required to save and stop young people and children from dying young or being locked in the pit of doom and injustice for the rest of their life with no parole in sight. We the People must always remember returning to having respect, love, justice and good intentions will be a real chance to rescue some young people and children from the consequences of gun violence and crime, because it's one hell of a fall off that cliff.

In 2010, gun violence and crime officially became a real true danger to young people and children living in our communities and neighborhoods. 2010 was a record-setting murder year, and it was also record-setting for the incarceration rates also known as the CONSEQUENCES. We have to promise our future generation that we will never break those records again, because it's bad for business of begging and cleaning up (Tourism). Young people and children have forgotten that killing is easy, but the hard part is living with it for the rest of your life in the pit of doom and injustice. IT'S HELL TO PAY.

Many young people and children see selling drugs or committing crimes as a quick way to make money, but they keep on forgetting it's a quick way to lose your life too, being killed or getting life in the pit of doom and injustice. We the People now have a generation of young people and children who are very violent and it's going to be very hard to straighten them out. They will take a gun and shoot and kill indiscriminately, because they don't care or give a damn about human life. The consequences of gun violence and crime continue to turn young people and children into the new jay birds locked in their cages for 23 hours a day, and that's got to be an unpleasant feeling for them.

These words or message is needed to help pull young people and children up on the consequences of their actions that sometimes lead to death or life in the pit of doom and injustice. Young people and children must never forget or realize it does not cost too much to have respect, love, justice and good intentions in their lives as their highest priority. The freedom and unity We the People now enjoy is slowly being taken away by gun violence and crime. If anyone needs proof, just buy and read a newspaper or turn on the radio or TV, and you will hear and see that the deterioration is now happening.

It's time We the People start looking for alternative routes from this planned doom of evil and injustice We the People have been on for too many years. We have to address all aspects of gun violence and crime and we can't do it all alone, without real help from politicians, high-ranking government officials, police officers and most of all religious leaders. They have forgotten that returning to having respect, love, justice and good intentions will be a vote of confidence that one day there'll be a real reduction in gun violence and crime. This vote of confidence has to be a unanimous one, because it's time for the condemnation of gun violence and crime evil regime. Gun violence and crime needs to be vigorously opposed every day by all the people who have been affected by a nonviolent or violent crime in the past.

In the 21st century, gun violence and crime now has no guidelines, it can happen anytime, anyplace, because there is no more respect and understanding in our communities and neighborhoods. Gun violence and crime has emerged as the king of the lawless jungle of injustice, evil and darkness a.k.a. planned doom. If this continues it will never make our communities and neighborhoods great again. Our communities and neighborhoods have been polluted with guns, drugs and ammunitions for decades, so it will be a real battle and fight to stop them from happening in the future. Thanks to the inaction by the people in charge, gun violence and crime continues to rise off the charts.

Some people now view gun violence and crime as a violation of their sovereignty, as the bloodshed continues to happen. The dire state of our communities and neighborhoods reflects the inaction and destructive attitudes and actions on the part of the people who are in charge, who are supposed to find solutions to this major problem. We the People are now fed up that gun violence and crime has spiraled out of control so fast, in just a short period of time. It has surrounded our communities and neighborhoods, like a black cloud, when it's time for rain. Gun violence and crime have a firm grip on power over our young people in children's lives, with no real end in sight to this serious problem. It's now the new messiah or boss for some of them, the ones who don't give a damn about any consequences, because they are now in neck deep in the waters of greed, disrespect, dishonor and disunity, which are the offspring of injustice, evil, and darkness a.k.a. planned doom.

The only way young people and children will learn this, is when they realize they are not supreme humans and life is not an Xbox or Internet game. When it's over, it's gone. You can't press restart. Young people and children must be taught to value every life, animal and human, as much as they value material possessions, drugs and doing what's not right. Gun violence and crime is so widespread that it's on the cusp of dislodging any hope We the People had in the recovery of having respect, love, justice and good intentions in our communities and neighborhoods. We the People need enhanced crime-fighting techniques that could be used against gun violence and crime because they continue to make mince meat of our communities and neighborhoods, while young people and children are dying or getting the worst consequences of any kind of life in the pit of doom and injustice (jail or prison).

We the People have to stop marching and walking because marching and walking without knowing the next step of attack to stopping gun violence and crime, is just people hanging out; or in the eyes of the people in charge, they look like troublemakers. We the People have to wake up and remember there is always power in numbers. If gun violence and crime continues to happen, it'll be time to write the obituary for communities and neighborhoods, because there will be no resurrection.

ONLY CONSEQUENCES!

MARTIAL LAW, COMING SOON!

GUN VIOLENCE AND CRIME VI
ONCE UPON A TIME
By
Mr. Dave R. Queeley

Once upon a time, all Virgin Islanders did not have to worry about gun violence and crime. Now in the 21st century, they have to worry about being robbed, raped and murdered for no good reason at all under the sun and moon. It's time for an immediate cease-fire, it's bad for business. The demise of gun violence and crime will only make the headlines, when all Virgin Islanders return to having respect, love, justice and good intentions as their highest priority in life and stop letting disrespect, dishonor and disunity be that priority. It's time to get rid of gun violence and crime in favor of mental and spiritual prosperity and unity. In the 21st century gun violence and crime now lurks around every street corner ready and willing to strike at any time. The decision on how to solve the gun violence and crime woes, cannot take any more backseat treatment. It's time for some real action because our future generation is dying and being locked up in the pit of doom and injustice for life.

The reduction of gun violence and crime would be an important achievement by the government system if they can get it accomplished. No more speaking out only on the condition of anonymity, because everyone is suffering, but it's still worrisome that these people want to continue to suffer in silence while the problem of gun violence and crime continues to get worse. In the 21st century, the digital era and connection has harmed instead of enhanced people's mental and spiritual awareness. It has siphoned away people's focus from the Creators original plan and Laws of Creation. The next generation is growing up with computers in their rooms with Internet hookup, cell phones and guns. To them these things are as much a part of their life as eating and sleeping. No matter what anyone says or does, being gangster is always on the mind, with the "No Snitching" philosophy running their lives.

Once upon a time, peer pressure did not influence young people and children into joining a gang or being a drug dealer and doing things they would not have done if it is wasn't for the pressure to fit in or to belong to something important. They now need positive interaction with their families, so that peer pressure does not continue to take control of their life and cause them to lose their life to gun violence or get a very long time in the pit of doom and injustice for committing a violent crime. Peer pressure is a monster society has to deal with if they want to see a decline in gun violence and crime. Unfortunately the criminal element does not broadcast their schedules when they're going to do some stupid shit. That's one of the main reasons why, we now need armed police patrols on a regular basis on our residential streets and not only where Satan and his angels of destruction live or hang out, continuing to plan peoples self destruction.

Gun violence and crime has turned the Virgin Islands into a cave for educated and lowlife criminals. Total self-destruction is not an imaginary threat anymore, it's now a fact. Gun violence and crime have a ripple effect on our communities and neighborhoods. Satan and his angels of destruction continue loving it when someone gets hurt or dies from a horrendous act of evil. Gun violence and crime is a deadly virus in our communities and neighborhoods that needs a cure to be eradicated soon. Gun violence and crime is something that is extremely hard to solve. It's something that some people think and believe we will never overcome, or find a true solution to stopping it from ever happening again in the 21st century. We the People need a new communication and crime-fighting strategy, if We the People want to see a real decline in gun violence and crime in our communities and neighborhoods.

These new strategies need to be unveiled as soon as possible, before it's too late for any action or solution to work. Still, our communities and neighborhoods remain vulnerable, especially since no one really knows how many illegal weapons are still in our communities and neighborhoods waiting to cause havoc or take another life. One possibility is, this problem will worsen and become a big headache for quite a while. We the People are going to have a lot of bullets to dodge in the future. The boldest move left would be for all Virgin Islanders to return to having respect, love, justice and good intentions as their top and highest priority in life. It will be the first step in the right direction in seeing the decline of gun violence and crime in our communities and neighborhoods. Having respect, love, justice and good intentions are at a historical low in some people's lives and they could care less if they live or die.

Gun violence and crime has dramatically deteriorated having respect, love, justice and good intentions in our communities and neighborhoods. This is a major problem to moving forward. Gun violence and crime has increased the hopelessness, dishonor and disunity in our communities and neighborhoods. It has been well documented by the newspaper, radio and TV stations. The last couple of years have been terrible. There is one thing that gun violence and crime brings to the table of life, which is the ability to not inspire young people and children to join the battle of good intentions over evil. The Creators original plan and the Laws of Creation is the furthest thing from their mind, body and soul; but a gun and how to commit a crime is always on their minds. They never think about the repercussions of their actions.

Once upon a time, the criminal injustice system (The Courts) was not for sale, but in the 21st century, once you have money to continue to grease the wheels of injustice, evil and darkness a.k.a. planned doom, you can do anything and get away with it; even red rum a.k.a. murder. These types of behaviors and actions continue to help with the deterioration of life in the Virgin Islands. Gun violence and crime is like the Energizer Bunny, it keeps on going and going with no real end in sight. It's at the disastrous level right now, and it can even be called a crisis. Some Virgin Islanders have grown very weary of the daily deterioration of life and the economical hardship that gun violence and crime has brought to the Virgin Islands.

Gun violence and crime is an evolving field of misery and everyone must strive to get a handle on what's the best solution to stopping it from ever happening again. Gun violence and crime is a great threat to We the People's mental and spiritual unity as Hitler's Nazis and Lenin's Communism was to the Jews. Stopping gun violence and crime will require a real sacrifice from all people, the wealthy and poor, to find real ways to fix this major problem. The wealthy lose their possessions and the poor lose their lives. It's the mentally and spiritually dead people are the ones who are responsible for gun violence and crime, not the gun. Gun violence and crime has eroded morale and unity among Virgin Islanders.

The unpredictability of gun violence and crime remains a serious concern to some people, and they are starting to conclude that they may never see a decline in gun violence and crime in their lifetime. It's time for the issues of gun violence and crime to be brought up on a regular basis every day. Virgin Islanders are not desperately looking for true solutions to the situation of gun violence and crime. They have forgotten that waiting too long, the situation will turn into a disaster with no end or help in sight, because Satan is the president of the institution of injustice, evil and darkness a.k.a. planned doom. Gun violence and crime are their offspring that continues to make our communities and neighborhoods a dangerous place to live and visit anytime. If gun violence and crime continues Virgin Islanders will never have the time to find the joy and happiness in life they used to enjoy...

ONCE UPON A TIME

Made in the USA
Columbia, SC
29 October 2024